JUDAISM

Published in the United States of America by Cherry Lake Publishing
Ann Arbor, Michigan
www.cherrylakepublishing.com

Content Adviser: Alexander Kocar, Princeton University

Reading Adviser: Marla Conn MS, Ed., Literacy specialist, Read-Ability, Inc.

Photo Credits: © goldnetz/Shutterstock, cover, 1; © Nicku/Shutterstock, 5; © Olan/Shutterstock, 6; © Lawrle Cate/
Flickr, 8; © Renata Sedmakova/Shutterstock, 11; © Freedom Studio/Shutterstock, 12; © Everett Historical/
Shutterstock, 14; © Peter Hermes Furian/Shutterstock, 16; © CREATISTA/Shutterstock, 19; © Robert Hoetink/
Shutterstock, 21; © Golden Pixels LLC/Shutterstock, 22; © Lucky Business/Shutterstock, 24; © Monkey Business
Images/Shutterstock, 27; © francesco de marco/Shutterstock, 28

Library of Congress Cataloging-in-Publication Data
Names: Marsico, Katie, 1980- author.
Title: Judaism / by Katie Marsico.
Description: Ann Arbor, Michigan : Cherry Lake Publishing, [2017] | Series: Global citizens: world religions |
    Includes bibliographical references and index.
Identifiers: LCCN 2016033584| ISBN 9781634721608 (hardcover) | ISBN 9781634722261 (pdf) |
    ISBN 9781634722926 (pbk.) | ISBN 9781634723589 (ebook)
Classification: LCC BM573 .M37 2017 | DDC 296—dc23
LC record available at https://lccn.loc.gov/2016033584

Cherry Lake Publishing would like to acknowledge the work of the Partnership for 21st Century Learning.
Please visit www.p21.org for more information.

Printed in the United States of America
Corporate Graphics

ABOUT THE AUTHOR

Katie Marsico is the author of more than 200 children's books. She lives in a suburb of Chicago, Illinois, with her husband and children.

TABLE OF CONTENTS

CHAPTER 1

History: Roots of the Religion

Since people began recording history, they have written about the idea of a power greater than themselves. Thousands of years later, various beliefs in God—or sometimes several gods—still shape human culture. Religion is the system people use to organize such beliefs. Religion also standardizes ceremonies and rules for worship.

God's Agreement with Abraham

Judaism, or the Jewish faith, is one of the world's oldest surviving monotheistic religions. Monotheism is the belief that there is only one true God. The history and legends about the Jewish people stretch back to about the 20th century BCE, and were recorded in writing. An important figure in the founding of Judaism was a man named Abraham, who lived in the ancient Middle East.

The ancient Hebrews were wanderers before settling in Canaan.

According to Jewish **scriptures**, also called the Old
Testament, Abraham was **righteous** and didn't worship any
false gods, or idols. God therefore chose to form a **covenant**, or
agreement, with him. As part of their agreement, God ordered
Abraham to journey into Canaan. This historic region was
located in southwestern Asia along the eastern part of the
Mediterranean Sea, near modern-day Israel.

God told Abraham that he would become the father of a holy
nation within the land of Canaan. In addition, God promised to

Moses led the Jews out of Egypt.

love and protect this nation's members—the **Hebrews**—in exchange for their faithfulness. It came to be understood that, if the Hebrews sinned, they would be punished for their actions. To them, the covenant marked the start of a special relationship between God and his chosen people.

The Early Israelites

Abraham served as the earliest patriarch, or father-like leader, of the Hebrews. He was followed by his son, Isaac, and Isaac's son, Jacob—who was also called Israel. As time passed, the Hebrews began referring to themselves as Israelites.

According to the story, **famine** eventually caused the Israelites to move to Egypt. At first, their situation improved, but then the Egyptians forced them into slavery. The Israelites waited for God to send a deliverer to free them.

During the 13th century BCE, the **prophet** Moses fulfilled this role. Jewish scriptures feature stories of God working through Moses to bring various plagues, or curses, upon the Egyptians. Ultimately, the Israelites were able to leave Egypt and head back to Canaan. Before they returned home, however, God renewed his covenant with them. He also gave Moses the Torah, which is Hebrew for "teachings."

Developing Questions

What does law have to do with religion? Why did the Torah play such an important role in the birth of Judaism? What other topics—besides the ones you just read about—does the Torah address? What exactly do the Ten Commandments say?

A compelling question doesn't have a clear answer but serves as an interesting discussion point. Supporting questions usually have more specific answers. Sometimes people use supporting questions to more closely examine compelling questions.

Jews live by the rules laid out in the Torah.

Guided by God's Rules

The Torah includes a set of 613 commandments, or **divine** rules. The Israelites believed God created these rules to guide their day-to-day lives. Everything from diet to family life was addressed within the Torah, which also contained the Ten Commandments. The Ten Commandments ordered people not to commit sins such as idol worship, theft, and murder. They also stressed the importance of obedience and loyalty.

In the Hebrew Bible, God communicated with Moses atop a

mountain in northeastern Egypt. Jewish scriptures mention how God carved the Ten Commandments onto two stone tablets. Moses later presented the tablets to the Israelites, who kept them in a sacred chest. Today, the exact location of this chest—called the Ark of the Covenant—is a mystery. What's clearer is that the stories of Abraham and Moses symbolized the birth of Judaism.

The 24 Books of the Jewish Bible

The name Torah also refers to the first portion of the 24-book Tanakh. This section of the Jewish Bible is made up of five books. The Torah contains a story of how God created the world. The Torah goes on to describe how Judaism and Jewish laws developed. The second section of the Tanakh—the Nevi'im—features eight books. The focus of the Nevi'im is the writings of the Hebrew prophets. The final segment is the 11-book Ketuvim. It is filled with a mixture of poetry, **philosophy**, and history. The Ketuvim was written between the fifth and second centuries BCE.

CHAPTER 2

Geography: Mapping How Faith Formed

Early Judaism was limited to areas in what are now Syria, Lebanon, Jordan, and Israel. Canaan stretched between the Jordan River and the Mediterranean. It was later split into the kingdoms of Israel and Judah and was later referred to as Palestine.

Starting in the 11th century BCE, Jewish prophets began **anointing** kings such as Saul, David, and Solomon. During this period, the Jews constructed a temple to worship God, as well as several palaces and public buildings. The temple was destroyed in 586 BCE, when Babylonian troops took over the city of Jerusalem. (Babylon was a kingdom in what is currently Iraq.)

The Jews rebuilt their temple, but they continued to face invaders. Syrians, Romans, and Arabs all seized control of Jewish

King David was both a writer and a warrior.

Christians believe that Jesus was the messiah, but Jews do not.

territory at various points. Sometimes they forced the Jews to relocate outside of their traditional homelands, in an **exile** called the Diaspora. The Diaspora was devastating to the people it impacted. However, it helped Judaism spread beyond the borders of what was once Canaan.

Beyond Middle Eastern Borders

By the **Middle Ages**, Judaism was no longer limited to the Middle East. Jews lived in Europe and Africa, too, though they often dealt with persecution, or poor treatment. They struggled for the right to practice their faith in areas where Christianity was the official religion. Christianity actually developed from Judaism between the first and second-century CE. It was based on the belief that Jesus of Nazareth—who was also Jewish—was the messiah.

The term *messiah* is Hebrew for "anointed one." Both Jews and Christians believed in the idea of God sending them his own

Gathering and Evaluating Sources

What's the best place to learn more about the geography of both ancient and modern Israel? Museums and cultural centers that focus on the history of the Jewish people are great places to start! Also talk to your teachers or parents about reaching out to nearby houses of worship. Finally, consider visiting your local library or heading online. (Be cautious—Internet sources are often helpful, but not all of them are reliable. If possible, try to use Web sites operated by government organizations or colleges and universities.)

Jews were taken from their homes and killed in camps during World War II.

chosen leader. They saw the Messiah as a powerful and important figure who could bring peace and justice by overcoming suffering and evil. Unlike Christians, however, Jews did not think Jesus was the Messiah. Even today, they say the Messiah has yet to arrive.

As Christianity spread across Europe, people who practiced anything other than the Christian faith were often viewed with suspicion. Centuries later, Jewish persecution would prove even more intense.

The Jews' Journey Home

During World War II (1939–1945), the **Nazi Party** carried out the killing of millions of European Jews. This mass slaughter was known as the Holocaust. Jews hoping to avoid persecution and death frequently fled countries under Nazi control.

Some settled in Western Europe, North America, South America, and Asia. Tens of thousands of other Jews escaped to the homeland of their ancestors. Decades earlier, many people who practiced Judaism had begun participating in organized efforts to return to Palestine. Such efforts increased as the Nazis steadily gained power throughout the 1930s.

A Look at Language

During the ninth century, Jews living in central Europe developed their own language—Yiddish. Eventually, Eastern European Jews began speaking Yiddish, as well. This language is based on German but is written with Hebrew characters. The Holocaust led to a decline, or decrease, in the use of Yiddish throughout central and Eastern Europe.

STATE OF
PALESTINE

Sea of Galilee

Haifa

Nazareth

I S R A E L

MEDITERRANEAN SEA

Hadera

Janin

Netanya

Tulkarm

Qalqilya

Nablus

Herzliya

1994 Treaty Line

West Bank

Jordan

TEL AVIV

Bat Yam

Ramla

Ramallah

Rehovot

Latrun Salient

Jericho

Ashdod

JERUSALEM **EAST JERUSALE**

Ashkelon

Bethlehem

Kiryat Gat

Gaza

Gaza Strip

Hebron

Deir al-Balah

1950 Armistice Line

1949 Armistice Line (Green Line)

Khan Yunis

Beer Sheva

Israel and Palestine have been in conflict for many years.

EGYPT

Dimona

Back in the Middle East, however, Jews became involved in conflicts over who actually owned Palestine. Arabs who had been living there considered the area their home. After the war ended, several world leaders suggested a possible solution: dividing Palestine into two nations. As a result, in 1948, the State of Israel was formed. It surrounds most of the Palestinian territories, except for the Gaza Strip—a narrow piece of land that is located on the Mediterranean between Israel and Egypt.

Today, Israel's population is primarily Jewish. Palestine is mainly made up of gentiles, or non-Jews. Disagreements about the borders that separate these nations still create tension between both groups.

CHAPTER 3

Civics: Organization and Ideas

According to recent studies, about 14 million people practice Judaism. These individuals represent approximately 0.2 percent of the world's population. Roughly 44 percent of them live in North America. Researchers say another 41 percent are found in the Middle East and North Africa. Europe is home to 10 percent of the world's Jews. The remaining 5 percent reside in Central America, South America, the Caribbean, Asia and the Pacific, and sub-Saharan Africa.

Religious Officials and Rituals

There is no central religious leader uniting people who practice Judaism. Rabbis, or teachers who are experts in Jewish law, usually head individual **congregations**. They oversee

Rabbis sometimes perform wedding ceremonies.

religious services at Jewish houses of worship, including synagogues and temples. Cantors are religious officials who assist rabbis. During services, cantors are responsible for singing or chanting prayers.

Every week, most Jews observe the Sabbath. This is the period from sundown on Friday to sundown on Saturday. The Sabbath is a time of rest and prayerful reflection. Jews often celebrate it by lighting candles and reciting prayers, songs, and blessings. Many also visit a house of worship and gather together for a family meal.

Different Denominations

Judaism is divided into three major subgroups, or denominations. These are Orthodox, Reform, and Conservative. The different branches of Judaism are often called movements.

Orthodox Judaism

Members of the Orthodox movement believe in strict obedience to the laws that God handed down to Moses. Most Orthodox services are in Hebrew, and men and women often sit in separate areas of the synagogue. Men also tend to play a larger role in religious ceremonies. Some Orthodox Jews dress like their ancestors did in 19th-century Europe. For men, this means dark

Developing Claims and Using Evidence

What led people who practiced the Jewish faith to split into different denominations? There are a few steps involved in answering this question. First, consider the similarities and differences between the four major branches of Judaism that you just read about. Use this information to form a statement answering the question above. Then prepare to do some research online or at the library or local houses of worship. Gather evidence to support the ideas in your claim!

Orthodox Jews wear traditional clothing.

Jews celebrate Hanukkah every winter.

hats and long, black coats. For married women, hats, scarves, wigs, or some type of head covering are considered appropriate.

Reform Judaism

Reform Jews concentrate on the **values** that religious laws teach. For them, this is more important than obeying every rule in the Torah word for word. A common belief they hold is that people should decide for themselves how important certain traditions are. Most Reform Jews are open to adapting, or changing, parts of their faith to keep up with the changing times.

As a result, they use both English and Hebrew to worship. Both men and women actively participate in public religious **rituals**.

Celebrating Faith

In Judaism, several holidays and festivals serve as opportunities for people to celebrate their beliefs. Some of the main Jewish holidays are described below.

Holiday	When It's Celebrated	Main Theme
Passover	March or April	Remembrance of God helping Moses guide the Israelites out of Egypt
Rosh Hashanah	September or October	Celebration of the Jewish New Year and the creation of Adam and Eve
Yom Kippur	September or October	Time for people to pray and ask God to forgive their sins
Hannukkah	Winter	Celebration that recalls the story of Judas Maccabaeus leading a military uprising against invaders

Note: Dates often vary, depending on the geographic location of individual faith communities and the practices within different denominations.

For many years, Conservative Jews did not accept women studying to become rabbis.

Conservative Judaism

Conservative Jews have beliefs that fall somewhere between the Orthodox and Reform movements. They're not opposed to people considering different interpretations, or meanings, of the laws that God gave to Moses. Yet Conservative Jews typically prefer to approach religious changes more gradually than Reform Jews. For example, they accepted the idea of women becoming rabbis and cantors in 1985. Overall, however, this practice sparked more **controversy** in Conservative Judaism than it did in Reform Judaism.

Reconstructionist Judaism

For Reconstructionist Jews, Judaism is not merely a religion—it is an entire civilization that is constantly developing. To them, this civilization is a reflection of the faith, history, literature, and day-to-day lives of the Jewish people. Reconstructionist Jews think of religious laws and traditions as opportunities to unite Jewish communities in the modern world. They do not view them as strict or unchanging guidelines.

CHAPTER 4

Economics: Funding a Faith

Like any other religion, Judaism is driven by the faith of its members. But individual congregations also face many day-to-day expenses that require economic support. Constructing and repairing synagogues, temples, and other buildings used for worship and religious education cost money. So does paying the salaries of rabbis, cantors, and additional staff.

Some Jewish congregations partner with local businesses and charities to perform community **outreach**. Many synagogues, temples, and **shuls** operate food pantries. Here, they offer free kosher meals and food items to people affected by financial hardship and hunger. (Kosher foods are prepared a certain way in order to uphold Jewish laws.)

Some Jewish organizations run food kitchens for the homeless.

Methods of Earning Money

A large number of Jewish congregations require dues, or membership fees, to cover their expenses. Dues are often calculated based on a family's size or members' ages. Alternately, certain synagogues, temples, and shuls say that people should pay 1.5 to 2 percent of their earnings.

Others don't ask for dues but send members letters of appeal. These letters request pledges, or promises to donate a set amount of money. In addition, congregations sometimes sell tickets for

The Western Wall, in Jerusalem, is one place Jews visit to pray.

Taking Informed Action

Religious persecution is not simply a problem of the past. Even today, members of several different faiths continue to struggle with unfair judgment, hatred, and violence. This includes people who practice Judaism. You can help end intolerance, or lack of acceptance. Make a list of major world religions such as Judaism, Christianity, Buddhism, Hinduism, Islam, and Sikhism. Next, research at least one major misconception, or incorrect idea, that people have about each. Think about why people have this misconception, as well as why they're wrong. Share what you learn with family, friends, or—if you belong to a certain religion—your own faith community!

reserved seating at houses of worship on major Jewish holidays. They generally pay for community outreach programs through donations and fund-raising efforts.

The Path of God's Chosen People

The support of its members is one of the reasons Judaism has survived so long. Despite countless challenges and centuries of persecution, their faith has remained strong. This strength is rooted in the belief that one true God decided to make the Jews his chosen people. It is the foundation upon which Judaism was born thousands of years ago. It is also what will undoubtedly continue to guide followers of Judaism thousands of years from now.

Communicating Conclusions

Think about what other costs are involved in the day-to-day operations of Jewish congregations—or any faith-based communities! (Hint: Keep in mind that synagogues, temples, and shuls are used for far more than worship. They also serve as learning centers and meeting halls where people discuss community issues.) Research this topic further. If possible, create a list or balance sheet showing the different expenses you learn about. Discuss what you find out with friends and family!

Think About It

According to a recent study, 35 percent of U.S. citizens who practice Judaism are part of the Reform movement. About 18 percent are Conservative Jews, and roughly 10 percent are Orthodox. Another 6 percent consider themselves Reconstructionists or members of smaller subgroups. Finally, 30 percent of Jews living in the United States say they're not connected to any particular denomination. Based on this data, what conclusions are you able to form? How would you guess these numbers compare to similar statistics in other parts of the world?

For More Information

FURTHER READING

Blake, Philip. *My Religion and Me: We Are Jews*. London: Hachette Children's Books, 2016.

Glossop, Jennifer, and John Mantha (illustrator). *The Kids Book of World Religions*. Toronto: Kids Can Press, Ltd., 2013.

WEB SITES

Akhlah—The Jewish Children's Learning Network
www.akhlah.com/
Head to this page to learn more about Jewish holidays, traditions, and history.

Chabad.org—Why I Like Being Jewish
http://www.chabad.org/kids/article_cdo/aid/1347962/jewish/Why-I-Like-Being-Jewish.htm
Visit this Web site to hear kids talk about why they enjoy practicing Judaism.

GLOSSARY

anointing (uh-NOINT-ing) choosing by divine election

congregations (kahng-gri-GAY-shuhnz) groups of people assembled for religious worship

controversy (KAHN-truh-ver-see) an argument in which people express strongly opposing views about something

covenant (KUHV-uh-nuhnt) a formal agreement to do or to avoid a certain thing

divine (dih-VINE) having to do with God

exile (EG-zile) a situation in which you are forbidden to live in your own country

famine (FAM-in) a serious lack of food in a geographic area

Hebrews (HEE-brooz) members of, or descendants from, one of the Jewish tribes of ancient times

Middle Ages (MID-uhl AY-jez) the period of European history from approximately 1000 to 1450 CE

Nazi Party (NAHT-see PAHR-tee) the political group that ruled Germany from 1933 to 1945; led by Adolf

Hitler, the Nazis killed millions of Jews, Gypsies, and others before and during World War II

outreach (OUT-reech) the extending of services or assistance

philosophy (fuh-LAH-suh-fee) the study of truth, wisdom, the nature of reality, and knowledge

prophet (PRAH-fit) a person who speaks or claims to speak to God

righteous (RYE-chuhs) without guilt or sin; morally good

rituals (RICH-oo-uhlz) acts that are always performed in the same way, usually as part of a religious or social ceremony

scriptures (SKRIP-churz) the sacred writings of a religion

shuls (SHUHLZ) synagogues

values (VAL-yooz) a person's principles of behavior and beliefs about what is most important in life

INDEX